Coming Alive at Cross
A 40 Day Adventure with Jesus

Jennifer Hand

Copyright © 2016 Jennifer Hand

All rights reserved.

ISBN: 978-1523856558
ISBN-13: 1523856556

DEDICATION

TJ ELLIS, YOUR FAITH INSPIRES ME TO PERSEVERE WHEN I WANT TO QUIT. THANKS FOR ALL THE AMAZING WAYS YOU TEACH ME ABOUT THE POWER OF THE CROSS.

CONTENTS

Acknowledgments
Forward
Introduction

1	Hope Beneath the Rubble	Pg 17
2	Baptized and Bold	Pg 33
3	An Invitation	Pg 45
4	Shepherd	Pg 56
5	The Sailor	Pg 66
6	Broken Bread and Betrayal	Pg 78
7	His Death My Life	Pg 88
8	He Came Alive	Pg 98

ACKNOWLEDGMENTS

This is one of my favorite parts to write in a book. The thanks. I feel all the feelings as I think about those who are a piece of this exciting journey called coming alive. I know this is a part of a book that not everyone reads, but I would love for you to read the names of those who have had a HUGE part of this adventure.

My Coming Alive Board of Directors are AMAZING. I am so beyond grateful that they said yes to this God-sized dream and I could not do it without them. Don and Debbie Sapp, Michelle and Todd Humbert, JP and Catrina Pruitt, Tresa Reeves, Justin and Brittany Smith, and Casey and Barry Lewis—I love you guys so much!

My Coming Alive Ministries Prayer team and book launch team. Thank you guys for saying yes and cheering this on, through your prayer and support.

Guys—you need to know I have the MOST amazing parents in the world. Mike and Vicky Hand thank you for all you taught me about Jesus and all you continue to teach me. I love you guys and am so beyond blessed to be your daughter.

And then there is my look alive- my twin sister Michelle Humbert. You are my best friend and womb-mate. I cannot believe God let me be born with my best friend. And then there is your hubby Todd Humbert. Thank you Todd for being the best brother ever. And your kiddos. I love being Aunt Nenn to Alex, Hope and Abbi.

Sherry and David Disney, I cannot thank you enough for taking me to Israel. This book is completely different because of that trip. What a life-changing trip. I love you both so much. Thank you for showing me Jesus.

And to the Israel family: Don and Darlene, Rocky and Linda, Shanda, Randy, Leslie and Robin—being in Israel with you guys was amazing. I love you guys.

And the anonymous donor who paid my way to experience the Israel trip. Words cannot express how much that impacted me. It changed me forever, and I know changed my ministry. Thank you for letting me SEE Jesus by walking where Jesus walk.

Casey Bagley, my editor. My victory sister. You are amazing. Thank you a thousand times over for taking these words and making them come to life. And YOU, my precious reader —thank you for taking the invitation to come alive!

FORWARD

Come alive at the cross.

Come alive at the foot of an instrument of death.

Come alive at the thought of someone else's death.

Come alive at the realization that death has been defeated, and you no longer have to live in fear.
This is the invitation extended to you. Your Heavenly Father invites you to find life through His Son.
I'm not sure I've met anyone who has come more alive through Jesus than my friend Jenn Hand.
When I read books I like to look up the picture of the author – sometimes on the back of the book; sometimes I have to search the interwebs. But I like to feel like I'm having a conversation with the author.
I encourage you to find a picture of Jenn. I have no doubt she will be smiling from ear to ear – most likely because she's cracking up at herself doing a photo shoot. Jenn never takes herself too seriously. That's just one of the many things I appreciate about her.
In the pages to follow, you will get to know this beautiful person who has found life in Jesus.
Don't worry about the author writing down to you from some high and lofty place; that's not Jenn. Now I will tell you, some of the stories Jenn shares will blow you away.
But they are true. Some of the things that have happened to Jenn...you just can't make this stuff up! She lives every moment, from the most embarrassing scenarios to the most profound opportunities.
Jenn's invitation to you and to me is find that very same life – to truly come alive.

We were created for this.
We were rescued from our sin for this. Don't just exist. LIVE!
Find freedom, find deliverance, find purpose, find joy. Laugh and cry.
Step out of your comfort zone and into adventure.
This is the invitation of the gospel.
This is what it means to come alive at the cross.

Blessings on your journey.

Jon Teague
Pastor Two Rivers Chattanooga

INTRODUCTION

Sipping strong iced coffee in my comfy clothes with the cutest dog at my feet and a napping baby beside me—this is how you would find me if you were wondering what the scene is like as I type these first words. Granted, I don't have a cute baby, or a dog, or a fancy iced-cold brew coffee making station. However, I do have the blessing of being a nanny for my best friend's baby and her dog one day a week. ("Nanny" sounds so much better than "babysitter," in my opinion.)

Sometimes, I think it is just nice to know the behind-the-scenes of writing. Here is another fact you should know - I was terrified to type the first sentence of this book. Well, any sentences actually. Maybe that is why I felt the need to start with something lighthearted...the image of the fluffy dog who looks like a giant teddy bear and the sweet baby sleeping beside me. I threw in the iced coffee because it was so tasty I could not imagine not mentioning it.

It also bears to mention that I am drinking ICED coffee in December because it is 75 degrees outside. In Tennessee. In December. That is crazy, folks.

I digress.

I was telling you about how I was scared to start. Do you ever have those moments when you know God is calling you to do something but you feel ill-equipped and nervous to obey – thinking maybe God meant to call someone, ANYONE besides me?

I have sensed God's calling in my heart for a while to write a 40-day devotional book that journeys with Jesus to the cross. The cross was an instrument of death. This instrument of death is the only way that I can ever truly find life.

The moments that led to the cross, the agony on the cross, and miracle of resurrection after the cross – these are the moments that change my life. That change your life.

These moments proved that Jesus was all that He claimed to be.

Jesus said to him, "I am the way, and the truth, and the life. No one comes to the Father except through me." (John 14:6)

Jesus came to earth as a baby. He was born so that He could die. Three days after He was buried, He came back to life.

He fought the chains of death for my life. And for your life. The impact of what happened on the cross the day Jesus willingly gave up His life is glory-shouting stuff, but sometimes it can become normal, everyday stuff.

Sometimes, it is easy for me to forget that He died so that I can live. Not just eternal life someday in heaven, but abundant life in relationship with Him today.

"I have come that you might have life and life abundantly." (John 10:10)

I don't know about you, but I do not want the miracle of the death and resurrection of Jesus to get swept into a place in my heart where I believe it happened but the weight of that happening doesn't change me. Daily.

It is because of the gift of the cross that I am redeemed, set free, forgiven, and can find life.

Lost

Have you ever found yourself lost? I remember the days when my dad had a giant atlas that was the road map he had to follow to get our family from Point A to Point B on a family trip.

I could not even figure out if the map was upside down or right side up, let alone try to read it to find direction. He was a great map reader. But there were the times when there was a detour, or he forgot the map, and he would try to find his way on his own. And then you would hear my mom sigh, quietly at first, then louder and louder, and finally she would say, "Mike, just stop and ask for directions!"

After those days came the Mapquest Days. That felt like big stuff to someone like me who could not read a map and was driving more, venturing to places I had never been before. You put in your starting address and your final destination, then printed off step by step directions telling you how to get there.

This worked well unless there was construction, or a detour, or you took a wrong turn and had no idea what to do next.

There was no GPS lady in a British accent telling you, "Recalculating."

I remember a particular time that I used Mapquest. I was raising support as a missionary and wanted to surprise one of my supporting churches and show up on a random Sunday. This particular church was a 3½ hour drive from my house. I had been there before, but with my terrible sense of direction, I was relying on Mapquest to get me there again.

I printed out the directions and set out to follow them. When I got to the church, it had the name of the church I was looking for. I thought it looked slightly different than I had remembered, but maybe I just had not had enough coffee that morning to be fully awake yet.

I walked in the church and quickly realized it was not the church I had been to before. That precious small congregation all turned to look at me with their beautiful, tall, church-lady hats and regal, well-tailored suits. I was most definitely out of place.

The pastor quickly came and warmly welcomed me and asked me what I was doing there.

I will never forget the moments that followed for the rest of my life. I wish I could tell you this story in person because it really was hilarious.

I told him I was a missionary who was planning on visiting another church but ended up at this church and was glad to join them for that day.

He said, "Well, HOONEY (it was drawn out in a beautiful southern way), do you pray to God?"

I assured him that I did enjoy praying to God.

He responded, "Well then, you can do our altar call today. Here is an extra robe and just come on and sit up front with me. And here is the can of Crisco. When they come for prayer, just grease them up!"

Yes. He gave me a beautiful robe to wear and a can of Crisco. And before I could say, "I have never done this before," we were at the front, sitting before the congregation.

I tried to sway with the music as gracefully as they did.

I tried to stifle the giggle that came deep from within my body, the

"I cannot believe I am at the 'wrong' church, but they are having this girl do the altar call" giggle.

Apparently, they wanted to do the altar call after the music. The pastor asked me to tell the congregation about myself before the altar call.

Keep in mind, I was used to speaking to quiet, pretty boring congregations. This congregation was fired up! I opened my mouth to say, "My name is Jenn," and the whole choir behind me plus the organ music played back, "Her name is Jenn!"

The music and the singing built with each thing I said.

I LOVED IT!

I think I ended up saying the whole country of Nepal where I was going to serve was going to get saved. That's how excited I got! It was glorious.

Then came the altar call. Everyone came to be prayed for by the random missionary girl who was still not quite sure what to do with the can of Crisco. So, as I prayed for them, I used it like anointing oil and made the sign of the cross on their forehead. I am so sorry if that was not the right thing. I just guessed.

Then, the pastor came forward and said something to me. He said, "Jenn, you may have thought you were in the wrong place at the wrong time, but God brought you here!"

And that church became a supporting church for my whole time as a missionary.

Why am I telling you this story? Because maybe you picked this book up and thought, I am not exactly sure why I am here. Or because, maybe as I writing this, I am wondering if I am in the right place at the right time.

I am not a big fancy theologian. The cross of Christ is a heavy topic. The power of Christ is something only the Holy Spirit can open our hearts to. It feels overwhelming to try to find words to carry the weight of the miracle that took place on the cross.

But I believe that you are not in the wrong place at the wrong time. I believe that God brought you here.

He brought me here.

To the cross.

To the moments of Jesus before the cross, on the way to the cross, on the cross, and after the cross.

And how those moments affect every single thing about my moments.

I believe God brought you and me here to spend the next 40 days on an adventure with Jesus.

Coming alive at the cross for the first time, or being reminded that, no matter how many times we have heard the story, it can transform our story anew.

We once were lost, but now we are found.

Coming Alive Together

I want to let you in on a secret. This book was already mostly written. I had poured hours and hours of quiet typing away in my little basement apartment. I spent most of the winter snuggled under a blanket, next to a heater, holding coffee, asking God to show me how to journey with you to the cross.

I set the publication date. I was ready. I kept coming to the open document to finish the book.

During this time, I clearly sensed the Holy Spirit whisper to my heart. You see, I had a trip to Israel planned in a few weeks. As I was drawing near to the date of leaving, I sensed the Lord's voice say, "I do not want you to write another word until you are in My land."

Well, glory!

So I paused, because I have learned that you cannot argue with the Lord. It's best to obey. And that gave me more time to pack!

Friends, those ten days in Israel changed me forever. I walked where Jesus walked. I saw where He carried His cross. I sat in the place where He sweat drops of blood for you and for me.

I saw, felt, and experienced Jesus there. And now, I come back to these pages. These words. As we see, feel, and experience Jesus here.

I am so excited about what God has in store for us as we come alive together at the cross.

The format of this book will be eight chapters with each chapter having five days of Digging Deeper Heart Work, ending in a total of forty days of Heart Work adventures with Jesus. These Heat Work sections will take you through chapters from all four gospels, and through the whole book of John. It is important to me that you know that the Bible speaks to YOU. Satan tries to tell us that the Bible is only understood by Biblical scholars. As you dig deeper into each heart work section, I want you to know that YOU are reading the Bible therefore you are a Bible scholar.

The Digging Deeper sections will include : Read It, Say It, Apply It, and Pray It. I will give you a section of the Bible to read, then a specific Bible verse to say out loud. I realize that may seem strange to some of you. But I believe there is so much power in speaking the Word of God out loud. It helps make it stick. It moves things from our head to our hearts. As you speak It, would you be so bold to put your name in the verse? Make it personal my friend, because we have a personal God.

In the Apply It section, I simply want you to have space to ask God how these verses apply to your life. How does knowing this about Jesus change you? How does this chapter speak to your situation?

In the Pray It section, I encourage you to write a prayer based on what God is speaking to your heart as you dig into the scripture.

There is also a space for Coming Alive Moments. This is just a space for you to record moments from the day that made you come alive. It's so much fun to notice these moments and remind ourselves Jesus is in the big and the little moments of our day.

I know there are some Type A folks among us. Then there are the slower, "let's just go at our own pace" types. So, I thought I would explain the format a bit for both of you.

Each chapter can be read at the beginning of the week if you want, then after finishing the chapter, you can start the five days of Digging Deeper for that chapter. I realize there are seven days in a week, but I only did five in case a day or two takes you longer, or in case you just want to take the weekend off.

Or if you want to—here is your permission to read EVERY chapter then start the forty days of Digging Deeper.

Or you can move at snail's pace and read a sentence here or there.

Truthfully, find a way that makes your heart come alive as you connect with Jesus.

And this would be such a fun journey to go on with a small group. Grab a group of friends if you want and come alive at the cross together.

Write in the book. Highlight in the book. Or get a fun journal and fancy pen and write your answers there. Just be You!

To truly come alive at the cross, we have to understand the One who carried the cross to die on the cross. Jesus. These chapters will take you on a journey of not just Jesus' death, but His life.

The cross is our hope.

The cross is our lifeline.

The cross is how we know our God is a promise-keeper. I cannot wait to come alive at the cross together.

CHAPTER 1 HOPE BENEATH THE RUBBLE

    The scene took my breath away. I had seen the pictures on CNN. I had pored over the posts of pictures from my friends who were living in Nepal when the 7.8 magnitude earthquake hit on April 25th, 2015. I knew there were hardly any other adjectives to describe the effects of the earthquake than "complete devastation." However, as I rounded the hill in Nepal two weeks later, I almost fell to my knees.

    Ten years before, I had come to Nepal as a fresh-out-of-college girl who really had no idea where the country was on the map. I only knew that it took a much too long plane ride, with your legs cramped in that tiny space, to get there. I was a travel rookie and did not know at the time I needed to request an aisle seat. The window seat seemed to fit my romantic traveling notions, as I thought I would love to watch the scene from that tiny window so far above the land below. What I was not taking into account was my small bladder (my friends once nicknamed me Tiny Tank) and that the man in the seat next to me would drink too much alcohol and basically pass out. Trying to gracefully crawl over a passed out man and the elderly lady next to him for your 1,000th bathroom trip is never the best idea.

    When our plane landed, I entered a world different in every way from the world I was used to. Our summer assignment as missionaries ended up vastly unlike my expectations. My team and I were assigned to work at the local hospital. My dreams of being a missionary nurse who changed the world could help me get excited about this "working at a hospital in Nepal" thing. Granted, I was not trained as a nurse, but I had watched a great many episodes of ER on Thursday nights, so that counted for something—right?

We were assigned the central surgical supply sterilization room. Our task—make maxi pads for the maternity ward. You read that right. For seven hours a day we would fold cotton and gauze together making maxi pads for the glory of the Lord. Changing the world, one maxi pad at a time.

(You can feel free to giggle here. It still makes me giggle to think about people's reactions at my supporting churches when I told them of our "oh, so glorious" missionary assignment.)

That summer was life changing for me. I got a parasite that I like to call Perry the Parasite. He left me very sick - like "spend all of your time in the squatty potty" sick. I was weak and weary and tired of making maxi pads. But God showed up in that little hospital sterile supply room. He taught me that, in my weakness, He can be strong. He taught me to love people when you are not even sure how to communicate with them. He taught me to love Him more. And He taught me to love a nation called Nepal.

If you had told me that summer that God would call me back to live in Nepal, I would have laughed. In fact, I told my mom on the phone once—after a hot, long day of making maxi pads with my friend Perry the ever-present Parasite—that I NEVER wanted to come to Nepal again.

But God.

But God called me back to live in that nation. He took my heart, broke it for the lost people of Nepal, and planted a piece of it right there in that country.

A few years later, I was appointed to work as a full-time missionary there. I learned the language, learned the people, and learned so much about God. When the time came for my assignment to end there, parts of my heart stayed behind.

It felt like time froze the morning I first saw my friend's post on Facebook:

It was pretty scary. We were all huddled together. I was praying, "Jesus you are our rock. Our strong tower. Ever present help in times of trouble" and thinking of what I wanted the last words I said to my children to be while I held them under my body. "Protect Clara, Jesus. She is my favorite thing. Jonah, he's my favorite thing. Protect them God." It was NOT a short quake but a long, long time of swaying back and forth as glass vases and frames shattered on the floor around us. Scary.

I read this post and immediately turned on the international news to find out what was happening in Nepal. I spent the next day poring over the news, seeing pictures of my old neighborhoods, the streets I had walked every day. I spent hours on the internet, trying to locate my friends and check on their well-being. Hours praying. Hours feeling helpless. And hours looking for plane tickets to get me back to the country that will always have a huge piece of my heart.

God opened the door wide for me to go, so I went. I know the language and have a Master's degree in counseling, so I prayed God would use me to help provide trauma debriefing for the Nepalese people that I dearly love.

That's how I found myself in the bouncy Jeep ride that day. I had just landed in Nepal the night before, so my body was not quite sure what day or time it was. My brain felt the fuzz of jet lag. As the Jeep bounced, so did my eyes. They bounced from place to place as I saw the pictures on the news come to life.

Entire villages destroyed. Children running the streets with the vacant look of trauma in their eyes. A three month old baby I held at the shop where we stopped for snacks whose mother and family had perished in the earthquake. The news quickly moved from my head to my heart.

But that holy hill is what really took my breath away, almost knocking me to my knees. We walked up a narrow path to the top of this hill. I almost felt I should take my shoes off as I stood on that ground - the sacred ground of unbelievable suffering.

The earthquake had occurred during church time. I was standing amongst the rubble of a church that had once held worshipers. They were singing and praising Jesus when the ground began to shake.

The church building literally looked like a pancake of rubble. I quickly learned that beneath that rubble, the bodies of eight people were buried. The pastor of the church had tried to pull his family out, but was only able to grab his wife's arm as the building collapsed around his family.

The pastor stood with us by the rubble, tears streaming down his face. His actual family and his church family were buried inside.

The remaining survivors were gathered under a small piece of tin right beside the rubble of the church. I was supposed to speak and offer them hope.

What words of hope could be offered there beside the rubble? Looking at a village that had no remaining buildings? Looking at a people that many had lost loved ones?

The first thing I did? I sat among them. Sometimes we just need to sit among the rubble—to be with them.

I love that we have a God who did that for us. He left the perfection of heaven to walk among us. Emmauel, God with us.

"Behold, the virgin shall conceive and bear a son, and they shall call his name, 'Emmanuel' which means, God with us." (Matthew 1:23)

Earth Shaking Moments

I am guessing you have experienced your own earthshaking moments. It may not have been in the form of a physical earthquake. It may have been that moment your family got a phone call that would change your life in an instant. It may have been a decision you made that you feel will leave you forever stuck in guilt and shame. It may have been a medical diagnosis given by a doctor in one of those small examination rooms. It may have been a job failure, a betrayal, or a broken relationship that finds you struggling to put together the pieces.

Perhaps it was a moment or a series of moments where you saw everything you knew, everything that felt safe and stable come crashing down. What do you do with the rubble? How can you find hope in the ruins? Can you find God in the story when it all comes crashing down?

I took one last look at the ruins of the church building before speaking with the people crowded under the tin shelter that day. As I looked, I noticed something. In the rubble of that flattened church, I could make out one thing. It was the cross. The cross which had stood at the top of the church. The cross was among the rubble.

The cross is an instrument of suffering that brought hope to a sinful and broken world. The cross stands as a symbol of a Jesus who understood suffering. A Jesus who was willing to take on suffering so that we could experience life - abundant life here on Earth and eternal life there in heaven.

"...looking to Jesus, the founder and perfecter of our faith, who for the joy that was set before him endured the cross, despising the shame..." (Hebrews 12:2)

Of course the cross would be among the rubble. That is the only way we can have hope in our suffering.

This moment was not the time for pat, Christian answers. You know the well-meaning answers people give when they feel the need to say something. Answers like, "God is working all things together for the good."

Yes, many times we know that, but when we stand beside the rubble, if we are gut level honest, that is a hard truth to hear in the moment.

In that moment, I just needed a reminder of hope. Those precious people I sat among needed a reminder of hope. And the cross—that was my anchor of hope in that moment.

Jesus knew suffering. In fact, He chose it so that my name and yours could be engraved on the palm of His hand.

"Beloved I have engraved your name on the palm of my hand." (Isaiah 49:16)

The pounding of nails pierced our names on His heart as He hung on the cross for us all.

After seeing the cross in the rubble, I stood to speak. I simply said something to the effect of, "We are with you. We are broken for you. We see you. We are praying for you. We are suffering with you."

And I held their hands. Their tears mingled with my tears. Our skin colors different but our hearts the same. Our hearts were somehow committed to clinging to hope together.

We had a time of prayer that I will never forget. In Nepal, when it is time to pray, everyone prays out loud at once, until someone ends the prayer.

This prayer time was ripe with raw emotion. The emotions of ones who had lost everything but were clinging to hope in something. They were clinging to hope that God and His goodness could be found there, somehow, in that rubble.

They cried out to God. It was real. It was heart-wrenching. But slowly, you could hear a theme throughout the prayers.

Dhanibhad Jesu. Thank you Jesus. They said this over and over.
They called on His name and thanked Him for the promises found in that name.

They were clinging to hope in the hopeless.

Can we go on a journey together to find this hope? To not ignore or stuff inside the raw, real emotions that come with the rubble of our earths shaking? To be filled with grace for each other as we walk on this holy ground of suffering?

I do not know what rubble you are in the midst of digging your heart out from under. I do not know what circumstance could have led you to search for hope in what may look like ruins.

I do know that the cross is our hope beneath the rubble, above the rubble, and around the rubble.

Power in a Name

I am going to switch gears with you for a moment. I want you to take a quick pause and think about your name. Do you know what your name means? Did you know in the tone of how your parents called your name if you were in big trouble and better start thinking now of ways to smoothly talk your way out of punishment? (I promise this has a point. Hang with me. Heat up your coffee if you need to.)

I have a twin sister. Identical twin sister, in fact. So identical that I cannot tell you which one of us is which in pictures of us from ages 0-14. Our cute little matching outfits could have something to do with that.

I was so often called by my sister's name, Michelle, that it became natural for me to answer. People had a fifty-fifty chance, so often they would just guess. And I would usually answer to either. I guess this gave me some sort of identity crisis.
In high school, I introduced myself once to someone as Michelle. The name rolled so easily off my lips, as I had answered to it so many times, that
I did not really even notice. Let's not even talk about when I filled out my voters' registration card at the registration table in the cafeteria one day.

Let's just say I may or may have not been distracted by the cute boy next to me, and I was watching Michelle fill her card out. I simply copied what she was writing. I have NO idea why. But that meant I wrote my name as Michelle Hand. Try having to explain that yes, you were intelligent enough to have the right to vote for the president, but you had written the wrong name on your card!

Being called by name is important. It identifies you. It is how you are known in a room.

Jesus was given a name by an angel when He was conceived in the womb.

"And Behold, you will conceive in your womb and bear a son, and you shall call his name Jesus. He will be great and will be called the Son of the Most High." (Luke 1:31)

When an angel tells you what to name your baby, and it's a virgin birth, I guess you feel obligated to listen and follow the angel's instructions. No need to pore over the baby books or pick the most popular name for the season.

Since I am not fluent in Greek or Hebrew, I had to do a little research. Jesus means "Yahweh saves" or "Yahweh is salvation."

In other words, wrapped up in the name of Jesus is the promise of our salvation. Salvation from our sins, our circumstances, our good days and our I-can-barely-get-out-of-bed days. Another element in the definition of His name is to deliver, save, or rescue.

There is great power wrapped up in the name of Jesus. There is no other name mighty to save!

Sometimes, I am tempted to want to save myself. To pull myself up by the bootstraps, whatever in the world that saying actually means. I have personally never worn bootstraps.

I want to will my way to survival in a situation. I want to clean up the rubble myself. I want to have the right emotional responses, be the rock, taking care of things on my own.

Would you please raise your hand and tell me I am not alone in this - wanting to have the perfect response to rescue myself out of situations when the walls come crashing down?

But the moment comes when I realize I cannot do this myself. I cannot say the perfect set of phrases and words to find healing. I cannot be strong enough, because the moment will come when the rubble of circumstance has buried my intentions.

I cannot deliver, save, or rescue.

In moments where life seems all shaky and there is nowhere to stand, I can feel free to fall. You can feel free to fall.

To call on the only Name that has the power to rescue, save, and deliver. To breathe it, whisper it, say it through sobs.

Jesus.

Jesus come.

Jesus meet me here.

Jesus hold me here.

Jesus sit with me here.

Side of the Road Shouts

I will never forget the night I received THE phone call. Maybe you have had a time where you answered the phone to a call you will never forget— the details etched forever in your mind and heart. I was in a town about 45 minutes away from my city visiting a friend, taking a 10:00 o'clock at night Sonic run, when the phone rang.

I answered because it was my pastor's wife, and it seemed odd that she would be calling so late at night. I had this feeling in my gut that something was wrong.

She said, "Jenn, there has been an accident." Immediately, my heart stopped, and I had to remind myself to breathe. She told me of how my twin sister, brother-in-law, five year old nephew, 9 month old niece, and a youth from the church were in this accident. The details were fuzzy at that moment, but we knew that they had been returning home from a youth group event. My brother-in law Todd was the church youth pastor and had taken the youth group bowling. As they were on their windy country road on the way home, there was another car traveling towards them. This car hit a deer that was crossing the road.

The car was going very fast, which propelled the large deer through the air like a missile. This deer hit my sister's minivan, flying through the windshield.

Todd does not remember what happened next, but apparently he saw the flying deer coming because he gripped the steering wheel so hard that he bent the steering wheel in half. The deer broke through the windshield, with Todd's face taking the full brunt of a 150 pound deer. Most of the bones in his face were broken. His eyes were filled with glass. The main artery in His neck was severed. His eye sockets were shattered. He was bleeding internally and aspirating on his blood.

His seat went backwards from the impact, which shielded my five year old nephew from the impact of the deer. However, Alex was conscious through the whole event, and still remembers it vividly. That is so much for a little five year old heart to take in.

The deer hit the ceiling of the minivan, and then fell onto my nine month old niece's car seat. Her car seat was knocked out of the base, flipping upside down, landing face down, with her brain and skull taking the majority of impact. She experienced immediate bleeding on her brain.

The deer then flew onto the backseat, landing in my twin sister's lap.

She had no idea what was happening. All she knew was that, in an instant, she had a very large animal on her lap, and she was covered in that animal's blood, mingled with the blood of her own family. The deer knocked her glasses off, and she could see nothing.

Somehow, she was able to grab her cell phone and call 911. She tried to explain to them that she was trapped, not by the vehicle, but by a large deer. When she heard her baby crying in the front seat, supernatural strength came over her, and she threw the deer off her lap.

She found herself on the side of the road. Her five year old son was covered in glass and deer fur, screaming, "Save my daddy!" Her nine month old baby was lifeless and unresponsive. Her husband was bleeding profusely, unconscious, and unable to respond.

Those were earth-shattering moments.

I will never forget what she told me she did on the side of the road that night. She said all she knew was to shout the name of Jesus. She whispered it, she sobbed it, she shouted it.

Jesus.

Jesus come.

Friends, I do not know what side of the road circumstance you find yourself in the middle of right now. I do not know what phone call has changed your life. Maybe your whole life has been a series of devastating circumstances.

I do know that we can always call on the name of Jesus. Side of the road moments or lifelong heartbreaks—we can rest in the power of His name. We can know that He is mighty to save, to deliver, to rescue. We may be questioning His method of deliverance and rescue—we will talk about that in later chapters. But in the heat of the battle, in the thick of the fire, I need to know that there is a name on which I can call, even when I can barely whisper it on my lips.

My name cannot save.

Your name cannot save.

My sister's vision was foggy because her glasses had been kicked off by the deer. Often in our difficult circumstances, it is very difficult to see clearly through the fog of fear, confusion, doubt, and despair.

We may not be able to see, but we can say the name of Jesus.

"For whoever will call upon the name of the Lord will be saved." (Romans 10:13, NASB)

If I can trust the name of the Lord for my salvation and eternal destination, I can trust the name of the Lord when everything is shaken. And if we are honest, in those moments, it's hard to trust in Him.

People do not often like to talk about it, but it's true. In our darkest hours, it can be so hard to trust what story He is writing.

If you are in that place of fear and distrust, God understands. He understands our questions and our fears—our wondering why these sentences of our life stories are being written this way.

I hung up with my pastor's wife that night, and my friend quickly headed to take me to the hospital. On our drive there, my sister called me from the ambulance. She was in the front of the ambulance, all the rest of her family in the back strapped to backboards. While I was talking with her, they upgraded to emergency status because Todd stopped breathing.

At that moment, I also stopped breathing.

And like my sister did on the side of the road, all I knew to do was call on the name Jesus.

I kept calling on His name as we pulled up to the hospital. I walked into the emergency room and saw what looked like the scene from a horror film, except it was my family, not actors. Deer fur, blood, and glass was everywhere. The emergency personnel said they had never seen anything like this.

I watched my sister's broken heart as her kids and her husband were in two different hospitals. I sat with my five year old nephew and held his hand as they vacuumed off the glass and cleaned his scrapes. I looked at my unresponsive niece and wondered if she would ever be the same again.

And I wondered when the earth would stop shaking.
And I called on the name of Jesus. Over and over and over.
I did not know what the end of the story would be.
You may not know what the end of your story will be.
But I knew I had to have a rock to stand on. A solid foundation to stand on.
And when I could not stand, a firm place to fall to the ground and kneel on.
On Christ the solid rock I had to stand. I did not have to understand His plan. I did not have to understand or know the outcome. I did not have to love the circumstance I was in.
But I knew in that moment, I needed a rock to cling to.
In all our moments, we need a rock to cling to.

"The Lord is my rock and my fortress and my deliverer, my God, my rock, in whom I take refuge, my shield, and the horn of my salvation, my stronghold." (Psalm 18:2)

I am praying that, in this moment, as you read these sentences, you can find hope—even if it is a thin thread.
Hope that you can call on His name.
Run to the name that is mighty to save.
To bring peace to your soul.

Jesus, who carried our cross, wants to carry you.

Heart Work Day 1

Read It: Read It: Matthew 1:18-23, Isaiah 9:1-6
Say It: (Don't forget to put your name in it) Hebrews 12:1-2
Apply It:

Pray It:

Coming Alive Moments:

Heart Work Day 2

Read It: Luke 1:26-38, Romans 5:1-11
Say It: Hebrews 6:19-20
Apply It:

Pray It:

Coming Alive Moments:

Heart Work Day 3

Read It: The cross is our reminder that there is hope beneath the rubble. We can cling to that hope. This hope is not just for when we feel buried underneath our circumstances. The cross also contains the promise of restoration and rebuilding. Let's read about the restoration that went on during the time of Nehemiah. Read Nehemiah Chapter 1 and Chapter 4.
Say It: Joel 2:25
Apply It:

Pray It:

Coming Alive Moments:

Heart Work Day 4

Read It: Chapter 1 reminds us that not only is there power in the cross, there is power in the name of Jesus. Read Mark 16 and experience the power of the resurrection. Specifically focus on Mark 16:14-20. What does Jesus say the disciples will do in the power of His name?

Say It: Philippians 2:7-11

Apply It:

Pray It:

Coming Alive Moments:

Heart Work Day 5

Read It: John 1:1-18 (You will read this again in a heart work day, but it is full of such powerful truth I want you to read it twice)
Say It: John 1:14
Apply It:

Pray It:

Coming Alive Moments:

2 BAPTIZED AND BOLD

On my recent trip to Israel, I had the opportunity to be baptized in the Jordan River. Now, I realize that each person reading this book comes from a different background. Different denominations, different churches, different beliefs about things. I am not writing this for us to get all defensive about baptism traditions.

Dunked, dribbled, drizzled, or poured, that's not what I want us to focus on here.

Also, can we not focus on the time I was speaking at a church that has a small podium-like thing that contained the baptismal bowl of water and I accidentally knocked it over, sending the water all over the choir below. I feel like word of stuff like that gets around—so can we just pretend that did not happen. The choir is still having a hard time recovering.

When I was learning the details of the trip to Israel, the trip leader informed us we could choose to be baptized in the Jordan River if we wanted. A small fee of ten dollars would rent our robe, towel, and give us a fancy "I was baptized in the Jordan River" certificate. I was hoping a coffee cup with the same saying came with the deal.

I decided that, if that water was good enough for Jesus to be baptized in, I surely wanted to experience it. And one of my favorite pastors, David Disney, was leading the trip, and what an incredible honor to be baptized by him.

We stood in line in our white robes that day. There was a nip in the air and quite the chill in the water, but my heart felt so warm. My sweet friend Sherry was leading the group in singing, "He is Here, listen closely. Hear Him calling out your name" as I walked into that water. All around us, people from different nations were worshiping in their language. Jesus says EVERY tribe and tongue will confess that He is Lord. What a place to watch that happen.

It was such a holy, sweet moment for me. As I was submersed under, all I could think of was how Jesus humbled Himself to be submersed in this same water.

When I came up out of the water, I was the same physically as when I went under, but my heart was changed. I was reminded of the death, burial, and resurrection of Jesus. I was reminded that because of His death, I am alive. And I was reminded I wanted to live for Him and not for Jenn.

It is Written

A pretty significant moment in the life of Jesus happened in Matthew 3. He was baptized by John the Baptist. John the Baptist had been hanging out in the wilderness preaching about repentance. Repentance is that fancy church word that sometimes I forget the gift and weight of the meaning of.

Repentance means "turning from my sins." To turn from my sinful ways, I really need someone to turn to.

That someone was the one John the Baptist and his locust-eating, camel hair-wearing self was telling everyone about. Jesus. And in Matthew 3, Jesus comes to John the Baptist to be baptized. I cannot imagine what that moment was like for John, but I imagine it was quite the powerful, humbling, life-changing moment.

I get Holy Ghost glory chill bumps (you know, the ones that make your tiny arm hairs stand on end) when I think about those moments when the Son of God, who created the waters that flowed in the Jordan River, was baptized in that river.

Immediately after being baptized, Matthew 4 tells us that Jesus was led into the wilderness. He fasted for the next 40 days and 40 nights during this time. It was during this time that Satan came and tried to tempt Jesus with all kinds of lies.

I guess he forgot who he was dealing with. Jesus refuted all of Satan's lies with these three little but power-filled words: "It is written."

Each time the enemy tempted Jesus with a lie, Jesus came back with the truth of scripture.

Have you ever noticed that any time you seem to have a special set apart experience with the Lord, the devil seems to enter the scene quickly with his lies?

He wants to distract us. He wants to confuse us. He wants to deceive us.

Did you ever go to the good old church youth camp? I loved my church camp days. Thursday night, the night before the last day of camp, was always my favorite. It was guaranteed you would sing the songs a little bit louder and with a little bit more passion, raising your hands a little bit higher, because it was the last night of camp.

The altar call would last a little longer. And then there were youth group devotions afterward. I always looked forward to what I knew would be a good old fashioned cry fest, with people confessing their sins and promising to rededicate their hearts to Jesus.

Spiritual high, mountaintop moments feel good. They bring heaven a little bit closer to earth.

And it does not have to be just at church camp or at a great worship service. It can be during a great time in the Word with your coffee cup and Jesus in the morning. Or while on a hike with God on a beautiful, sunny day.

These moments are gifts.

But just like after Jesus was baptized and taken to the wilderness, we can quickly find ourselves leaving the mountain and in the valley. And I want to fight the lies of Satan in my own wilderness times just like Jesus did. With the truth of what is written in God's word. Jesus had been baptized, and He was walking boldly.

Mistaken Identity

Have you ever mistaken one thing for something else?

Just this week, I made a pretty big mistake. It was tooth brushing time. Truth be told, I hate to brush my teeth. Don't worry, I do brush my teeth. In fact, you can always tell when I have squeezed a tube of toothpaste according to my roommates.

I thought I was being all sneaky one time when I ran out of toothpaste and I was using my roommate Casey's. That is until she laughingly told me she could tell every time I used her toothpaste because I squeeze the tube hard from the middle.

Go big or go home.

I digress.

I hate to brush my teeth. This particular morning, I could not find my glasses, and I was not ready to put my contacts in quite yet, since my eyes were barely opened. The worst thing about being almost blind as a bat is when you have dropped your glasses somewhere underneath the bed when you fell asleep watching

Netflix. I have been known to whisper desperate pleas to God to help me find those glasses that have been around so many years they do not even sit straight on my face.

Since I could not find my glasses, I went to the medicine cabinet and decided to brush my teeth. Clean teeth, clear eyes or something like that.

So, I grabbed a tube, squeezed on my toothbrush and started to brush away.

My lips quickly started to tingle, my mouth went numb, and I could barely contain my gag reflex.

I may or may not have brushed my teeth with Benadryl cream. Hey, it happens to the best of us, right?

I mistook one thing for another.

John 1:19-28 tells us the story of John the Baptist. His story is amazing. He was the result of a miraculous fulfillment of answered prayers for his mom and dad. You can read all about how his barren mom

Elizabeth found out she was pregnant with him in Luke 1:5-25. John's birth took away Elizabeth's shame among the people.

Back in those days, to be barren was a shameful experience. If you could not provide a namesake for your husband's family line, people talked about you behind your back, or to your front. They wondered what sin you had committed that kept you from having children.

> *"Thus the Lord has done for me in the days when He looked on me, to take away my reproach from the people." (Luke 1:25)*

John's purpose on earth was proclaimed before he was even born. He may have taken away the shame of his mother, but his purpose was to proclaim the message of the One coming who would take away the shame of the WHOLE world.

The angel told Zechariah, John's father, that John would turn many of the children of Israel to the Lord their God.

John was doing ministry in the wilderness. People were coming to him to be baptized. It seems like many people were mistaking him for the Messiah. It can be so easy to mistake one thing for another. They probably wanted him to be the Messiah they were looking for. They wanted being baptized by him to baptize them right into heaven.

I imagine they may have wanted to worship him. In fact, they kept asking who he was (John 1:19).

It is so easy for us to mistake one thing for another, spiritually. Mistaking "performance for God" for worship of God. Mistaking people's approval for God's approval.

Believing that more things, more perfection, more pounds lost, more perfect parenting, more perfect relationships will lead us to fulfillment and satisfaction.

John wanted to make sure that they did not mistake who was the Messiah. He did not want them to exchange one thing for another.

John speaks a very powerful statement in John 1:29.

"The next day he saw Jesus coming toward him and said, 'Behold, the lamb of God, who takes away the sin of the world.'"

He wanted to make sure the people made no mistake. This was Jesus. The One who would set them free from sin and shame.

Friends, where are we missing Jesus? How are we mistaking other things, people, or circumstances as things to take the place only Jesus can fill?

Come alive at the cross today recognizing who Jesus is – the Son of God who takes away the sin of the world. Who takes away the sin of our hearts. Behold the Lamb of God.

Worth Following

Have you ever tried to be all sneaky and follow someone? I am frankly not good at being sneaky or at surprises. So, I cannot say that I would make a very stealthy follow-someone-and-they-do-not-know-it girl.

I mean, I give myself away playing hide and seek with my nephew and nieces. Like they are the adults and I am the seven year old or five year old. They come looking for me. And I have picked the BEST hiding place. But I cannot help it. I giggle and giggle, and they know exactly where I am. (Yes, I am 33, and I am still bad at this game!)

I think maybe it comes from a traumatic experience in my youth group days. We used to play a game called Sardines, which is like Hide and Seek but way more fun. You find a hiding place, and then everyone else is looking for you. If they find you, the get in the spot with you. (The smaller the better, right? Well, at least it makes for more giggles).

Our youth group met in a really old church building. There were all kinds of creepy, small, dark hiding spaces. I was picked as the one to hide (probably because, as stated above, I was the EASIEST to find). I hid in this small space and waited. And waited. And waited.

And no one came.

I tried to wait it out but I had to go to the bathroom. So, after what felt like three days (in reality was probably only 6.5 minutes), I left my spot to find all my friends outside.

That really does not have anything to do with the story, but talking about being sneaky made me think of hide and seek. Hide and seek brought me back to that traumatic moment, and I just felt like I needed to process it with you.

Thank you. I feel better now.

John 1:37 tells us how two of John's disciples heard John declare Jesus to be the Lamb of God. They must have felt that was a pretty significant title to give someone, so they decided to be sneaky. They decided to follow Jesus.

Well, He's Jesus. So don't try to sneak around on Him.

They recognized something in Him worth following.

He recognized something in them, too. He recognized they were followers.

I find it funny that when He asked them what they were seeking, they asked Him where He was staying. And He said, "Come, and you will see."

Come in. Come to my place, and you will see.
And see they did. They said they had found the Messiah, which means "Christ."

Seek and you shall find. He does not hide when we seek.

Jeremiah 29:13 says "You will seek me and find me, when you seek me with all your heart."

We seek and He does not hide. He crawls into those places - those places where we have tried to hide. He does not leave us there alone.

The cross was His way to find us. The cross is our way to find Him. The cross is how we recognize He is our Messiah, the One who saves.

"For the Son of Man came to seek and save the lost." (Luke 19:10)

I said the Sardines Hide and Seek gone wrong story didn't have anything to do with anything, but really, it does.

The point of Sardines is that the people that are looking for you come and find you. And when they find you, they get in the small, dark hiding place with you.

Jesus came to find us. To get into the places where we try to hide our sin, where we try to cover up. The darkness.

And when He found us, He got in that place with us. He took on sin FOR us.

"Surely He has borne our griefs and carried our sorrow; yet we esteemed him stricken, smitten by God and afflicted. But he was pierced for our transgressions; he was crushed for our iniquities; upon him was the chastisement that brought us peace, and with his wounds we are healed." (Isaiah 53:4-5)

It was and is a search and rescue mission. And He rescues us because He delights in us (Psalm 18:19).

I want to be like the disciples that day. I want to FOLLOW. I do not want to hide.

Behold the Lamb, who takes away your sins. Follow Him. Come with Him.

Come alive in Him.

Heart Work Day 6

Read It: Read Matthew 3
Say It: Matthew 3:11-12
Apply It:

Pray It:

Coming Alive Moments:

Heart Work Day 7

Read It: Matthew 4:1-17
Say It: Matthew 4:4
Apply It:

Pray It:

Coming Alive Moments:

Heart Work Day 8

Read It: John 1:1-34
Say It: John 1:16
Apply It:

Pray It:

Coming Alive Moments:

Heart Work Day 9

Read It: John 1:29-51, John 2
Say It: John 1:48 (put your name in place of Nathanael) He sees you and calls YOU.
Apply It:

Pray It:

Coming Alive Moments:

Heart Work Day 10

Read It: John 3
Say It: John 3:16-17
Apply It:

Pray It:

Coming Alive Moments:

3 AN INVITATION

When did you first accept your invitation to come alive in Christ? I really wish that I could sit with you and hear all of your answers. If you have not accepted your invitation to come alive in Christ, consider this an invitation with your name on it.

I was a grow-up-in-church kind of girl. My parents shared Jesus with me. The nursery workers shared Jesus with me. The VBS teachers shared Jesus with me.

It was Psalty the Singing Songbook, a giant hymnbook that sang kid songs, who led me to really want to know Jesus. He was singing about mansions in heaven, and I wanted to make sure I had one. (So super spiritual, huh?)

But really—I did have that sense of stirring that I wanted Jesus to be my best friend at a very young age.

I wrote in my perfume scented diary these words: "Dear diary, I want to know Jesus."

I then placed that oh-so-secret key to my heart-scented diary on my parent's bed.

The next thing I knew, my pastor's wife at the time, Sharon Belva, came to our house to share with my twin sister and me what we needed to do to accept this invitation to life in Christ.

The glorious truth I learned that day is that the only DOING that is required is really more of a BEING. BElieve.

Believe that Jesus died for sinful me. That He died for a relationship with me. And that eternal life was offered as a free gift of grace for me.

That night, I sat on the couch with Mrs. Belva and was led in a prayer that changed EVERYTHING. (Side note: Years later, in high school, Mrs. Belva was my typing teacher. She taught me how to type. Not only did she lead me in the prayer that changed my life, she gave me the skills to type these words to you. If there are typos, that is NOT her fault).

You may have been eight years old or eighty years old. Twenty-two or thirteen. (Yep, I am picking random numbers here, folks.) Or it may be that you sense Christ calling your name in this very moment.

John 1:14 says, "...and the Word became flesh and dwelt among us, and we have seen his glory, glory as of the only Son from the Father, full of grace and truth."

To come alive at the cross, I want us to study the steps of the Christ who carried that cross.

The One who became flesh and dwelt among us so that we can see God's glory.

The Creator came to commune with the created.

Accepting this invitation, it really is an adventure. Sometimes I can forget that, and I wonder if you can too? We can let the stories of Jesus become normal and every day, forgetting that Jesus' steps on earth change everything about our days.

There is nothing everyday about heaven breaking forth into earth. In that breaking, the curse of sin was broken.

The invitation is to come alive, not just in eternity, but in our everyday.

John 1:16 says, "From His fullness we have all received grace upon grace."

I like things in excess. This weekend was Valentine's weekend. I found that to be a perfectly good reason to enjoy an excessive amount of sweets. My friend, Becca, bought this delicious hot-out-of-the-oven blueberry cobbler to our small group last night, and I enjoyed every bite of this Valentine treat. And then some more bites. And more.

Our God is an excess kind of God. I love that the word grace in John 1:16 was not just used once. It was used twice. He wanted to give us an extra measure of grace.

When I looked at the definition of excess, it means "an amount of something that is more than necessary."

Wow. Grace upon grace.

More than necessary.

As we study the footsteps of Jesus, let's wrap ourselves up in this grace. Sometimes, we can fear that if we focus on grace, we will let sin abound. Paul questioned that himself.

Romans 6:1 says, "What shall we say then? Are we to continue in sin that grace may abound? By no means!"

Grace is a gift that can direct us to wanting to return the gift by living FREE. We die to sin so we can live.
Come alive at the cross in grace today.

Thirsty

I am sipping a delicious, hot Americano with steamed cream right at this very moment. I am also wearing a shirt that says, " Ok, but first coffee."

Hello, my name is Jenn, and I am slightly obsessed with coffee. It started out with the little packets of cappuccino they gave us in church youth group to keep us awake in seventh grade Sunday School class. Then, in high school, my Dad further added to my love of coffee when he started a coffee shop ministry for high schoolers to come to on Friday night, hang out, play pool, and hear about Jesus. Someone donated a whole tractor trailer load full of this cappuccino called "Killa Vanilla."

My coffee journey continued in college. (Why do I feel like I am giving you my coffee testimony here?) I blame my best friend, Casey Lewis, for my learning to drink the "hard stuff." She gradually taught me to drink my coffee stronger and stronger.

Now, I like it best when it resembles motor oil.

The truth is, though I love coffee, it does not quench real thirst. It was not created to.

When our bodies are thirsty, they are really craving water.

Have you ever been thirsty? The "all I can think about is an ice cold glass of water" thirsty? Imagine a moment after extreme exercise. Truthfully, it's been a while since I have done any extreme exercise. Well, I did just do a back bend to try to grab my pen that fell. But, I am thinking that does not count. (I feel the need to insert here that I ran a marathon once. I try to insert that in stories as often as I can, and this seemed like an appropriate place to do that!)

Imagine that moment when you are exhausted. You have given everything you have. Your body is tired. Your throat is parched and dry. And someone comes and offers you a giant glass of ice water. Don't just stand there...drink up my friend. Let the water pour down your dry throat.

Settle in. I can almost hear the sound of satisfaction... AHHH. Ok, I know I got a little imaginative there on you guys for a second. But hang with me.

Truthfully, our physical bodies are not the only things that thirst. We have a deep, soul thirst. A heart that is thirsty for love, for acceptance, for being known.

A heart that is thirsty to worship something.

John 4 tells us a story about thirst. Jesus had been traveling from Judea to Galilee. He had to go through Samaria, and in the middle of His journey, He got thirsty and sat down beside a well.

Honestly, thirsty or not, I believe Jesus chose that exact well because He knew who was coming to draw water.

> *John 4:7, "There came a woman of Samaria to draw water. Jesus said to her, ' Give me a drink.'"*

A side note that you should know: In Jesus' time, Jews and Samaritans did not mingle. It would have been strange for Jesus to talk to a Samaritan.

Even more significant, she was a Samaritan woman.

Jesus did not let cultural norms stop him. He asked the woman to give Him a drink. She pointed out to Him that maybe He had forgotten the social rules at the time.

> *John 4:9, "The Samaritan woman said to him, 'How is it that you, a Jew, ask for a drink from me, a woman of Samaria?'"*

Jesus then tells her if she knew who He was, she would have asked him for living water.

This has the makings of a reality television show friends. She responds with a questioning heart. Tell me what this living water is. You do not even have a bucket here to get water.

Jesus' response to her questions in verse 13 and 14 of John 4 hold significant answers for our own soul thirst.

> *"Everyone who drinks of this water will be thirsty again, but whoever drinks of the water that I will give him will never be thirsty forever. The water that I will give him will become in him a spring of water welling up to eternal life."*

I just want to take a second and shout GLORY!

My soul thirsts for people to notice me. For people to love me. For approval. To be enough.

I can try/have tried a thousand different ways to quench that thirst, but it doesn't work.

I do a great job at something, but then fail at the next thing—thirsty again.

Someone tells me they are impressed by me, but then someone else points out a failure—thirsty again.

I do a great "service" for Jesus, but then I turn around and gossip about the people I served with—thirsty again.

You insert your own thirsty moments.

We can try and try to draw water from an unquenchable well, but somehow, some way, we will always end up soul thirsty.

BUT Jesus.

Jesus offers us a water that springs up. That offers eternal life. That promises I will never be thirsty forever.

Jesus came to the woman at the well that day. He comes to you today. And every day. His mercies are new for you anytime you want to drink from them.

I love the woman's response. She said, "Sir, give me this water, so that I will not be thirsty or have to come here to draw water."

I want to come to Jesus and say, "Jesus, give me this water. I am trying to quench my thirst here on earth with other things. Forgive me for forgetting. Would you quench this thirst?"

Thirsty no more.

Jesus goes on to tell the woman something she was maybe hoping He would be the one person in town that day that didn't know. That did not know that she had had five husbands and that the man she was with now was not her husband.

Did I mention reality television show?

He told her about her sin in a way only Jesus can. Without condemnation. He offered her this living water knowing her. Knowing everything about her. He knew the thirst in her soul. He knows the thirst in our souls.

He knew that He was on earth for one reason. To seek and save the lost. To carry a cross so He could carry the weight of their sin. Of her sin. Of my sin.

He offers living water.

I was blessed to be able to visit that well when I was in Israel. There is a church built around the well, but it is the original well that Jesus would have sat on waiting for the woman.

I imagined him sitting there waiting for me. Would I take the living water?

When I was standing by that well, I reached down and dipped some water. There was nothing miraculous in the water. The miracle was in the one who had offered the water.

He came that I may find life. He came that I might find freedom from sin. He came that I may thirst no more.

Would you take your soul up to that well today? Maybe you are tired of trying and failing. Maybe you are lonely. Maybe you are wishing you were living someone else's life story. Maybe you have been a Christian so long that you have forgotten what a gift that living water is.

However you find yourself today, would you meet Jesus at that well? Would you let Him offer you a drink?

Heart Work Day 11

Read It: John 4:1-44
Say It: John 4: 13-15
Apply It:

Pray It:

Coming Alive Moments:

Heart Work Day 12

Read It: John 5-6
Say It: John 6:35
Apply It:

Pray It:

Coming Alive Moments:

Heart Work Day 13

Read It: John 7
Say It: John 7:38
Apply It:

Pray It:

Coming Alive Moments:

Heart Work Day 14

Read It: John 8
Say It: John 8:11
Apply It:

Pray It:

Coming Alive Moments:

Heart Work Day 15

Read It: John 9
Say It: John 9:3-5

Apply It:

Pray It:

Coming Alive Moments:

4 SHEPHERD

I remember my Precious Moments Children's Bible so well. It was given to me as a gift when I asked Jesus to be my Savior. The pink, fake leather is cracked and worn, as I loved that Bible. I poured over the pages. Jesus became my best friend in those pages that had Bible passages illustrated with Precious Moments figurines. (If you happen to not know what a Precious Moments figurine is, Google it for an illustration.)

I used to make my friends skip out on playing on the playground but instead come to the Bible club I taught from that Bible. I thought we were having quite the revival, with kids coming to know Jesus right and left.

It could have been they wanted to accept Jesus so they could go swing.

One of the pictures I most vividly remember was with Psalm 23. Even if you are not familiar with the Bible, there is a very good chance you are familiar with Psalm 23. In that Bible, the illustration contained the sweetest looking shepherd (those Precious Moments have giant, almond-shaped eyes) with his little sheep by a stream, holding a giant shepherd's hook.

Let's be honest - we do not see that many shepherds around in our normal life. So this was the picture I had of a shepherd. And truthfully, when I thought about Psalm 23 opening with the line, "The Lord is my shepherd," I equated it with the "funeral passage."

This is a passage read at many funerals. I can almost hear the organ music pumping in the background.

"Even though I walk through the valley of the shadow of death, I will fear no evil." (Psalms 23:4)

There is something to these shepherd analogies. In John 10:14, Jesus declares, *"I am the Good Shepherd."*

What does that really mean for us, who do not have a group of sheep following us wherever we go? How do we enter into the weight of the promise that Jesus is our Shepherd? And what does this have to do with the promise and the power of the cross?

Would you dive into John 10 with me? P.S. People must still get excited about sheep. Last week I posted a selfie of me and a sheep at a petting zoo. That picture had more likes than anything I have posted in a while. So let's get excited about being a sheep.

I am the Good Shepherd

I am not a good shepherd. When I was living in Nepal, my teammate and I bought a goat (which I do realize is a whole different animal than a sheep, but it is as close as I can get). We had jokingly stated that if we could get our visas renewed to stay in the country (things were not looking good at that point), that we would buy a goat.

We knew nothing about goats. I had never even had a pet dog for goodness sakes.

We got our visas, so we got our goat. We named it Baggy (pronounced baagy not baggy) named after the stinky Bhagmati River. Public service announcement for you - Goats stink!

Baggy did not like living alone. Apparently, goats like friends.

Our Nepalese friends were also determined this goat should live in our living room to stay warm. We were not so much keen on that idea, so we had what I called the Goat Mahal (after the Taj Mahal) built.

But one day, I walked out, and Baggy had gotten its little head wrapped around his rope, and he was not breathing.

I did what everyone would do. I did mouth to mouth on that goat. And he lived!

That was the end of my shepherding skills.

In John 10, Jesus declares to us that He is the good shepherd. What was the role of a good shepherd? A good shepherd kept his sheep alive. A good shepherd watched for enemies that were coming to kill his sheep. A good shepherd took his sheep to the resources they needed. A good shepherd led his sheep safely, looking out for obstacles along the way. A good shepherd watched for injury. A good shepherd provided for his sheep.

Jesus keeps our souls alive. Jesus watches for the enemy who comes to steal, kill and destroy (John 10:10). Jesus provides everything we need. Jesus leads us. Jesus looks out for obstacles. Jesus heals us when we are injured. Jesus provides for us—His sheep.

"I am the good shepherd. The good shepherd lays down his life for the sheep. He who is a hired hand and not a shepherd, who does not own the sheep, sees the wolf coming and leaves the sheep and flees and the wolf snatches them and scatters them. He flees because He is a hired hand and cares nothing for the sheep. I am the good shepherd, I know my own and my own know me, just as the Father knows me and I know the Father, and I lay down my life for the sheep." John 10:11-15

Jesus is no hired hand. His hands were present at creation. In the beginning was the Word and the Word was God.

John 1:14 says, "and the Word became flesh and dwelt among us."
The One who formed the heavens and earth walked the earth.
He invested HIMSELF.
He lay down His life for His sheep. He looks for His sheep.
Jesus was teaching the disciples in parables in Mathew 18. He shares with them the parable of the lost sheep.

"If a man has a hundred sheep and one of them has gone astray, does he not leave the ninety-nine on the mountains and go in search of the one that went astray?"

Jesus came to seek and save the lost.

He came for me. He came for you. And He is still searching for the ones who have gone astray.

Let that sink in. What a personal loving Savior we have. He sacrificed His life for His sheep.

He came looking for us.

I once was lost but now I am found.

Let's go back to Psalm 23. When I read this Psalm, I always pictured a lush, green pastureland. And a shepherd that looked like the picture in my Precious Moments Bible.

On my recent trip to Israel, I saw shepherds everywhere. That was one of the highlights of my trip. I was looking for them and their sheep. I wanted them to be wearing long white robes, but the modern shepherds of today tended to have on jeans and a t-shirt. They also tended to be smoking cigarettes, but hey, we will just pretend they were not smoking shepherds and that they were still in long, white robes with staffs in their hands.

We drove past Galilee into the "sheep land" as I called it. These were some crazy rolling hills. Not the flat pastures that I had expected.

The guide came over the loudspeaker and told us we were going to be going to the area they called the "valley of the shadow of death." The scene there took my breath away. I can no longer read Psalm 23 with the pleasant, green pastureland as the scenery backdrop.

This place they called the valley of the shadow of death was huge cliffs overlooking a very, VERY deep valley. The paths on the side of these cliffs were small and filled with precarious stones.

This is what Psalm 23 was talking about.

"Even though I walk through the valley of the shadow of death, I will fear no evil. Your rod and your staff, they comfort me."

If they started to fall, the shepherd would have to rescue them with his staff.

The sheep would have had to closely follow their shepherd into this deep valley. At the bottom of the valley is where the water was. It is where they would find the refreshment they needed. The small, precarious paths leading through to the valley are called the paths of righteousness.

This would not have been an easy journey for a sheep. They could not have decided to go their own way. They had to follow their shepherd and the shepherd had to be trustworthy.

I don't really like to use the word "stupid," but let's be honest, sometimes I can be like a stupid sheep. I want to make my own path.

I find myself injured, and I think I can take care of it myself. I want to trust my own ideas, my own plans, my own ways. Sometimes the direction the Lord is leading me seems terrifying. I think maybe the other "pasture" looks much greener. Sometimes, I can think maybe God is making a mistake in the path He is leading me.

Please tell me I am not alone here in those feelings, friends?

Psalm 119:105, "Your Word is a lamp to my feet and a light to my path." Psalm 18:33 "He made my feet like the feet of the deer and set me secure on the heights."

He will lead me. He will guide me. He will protect me. I can lean in and fully trust. What a good Shepherd.

The shepherd used his staff to rescue a sheep when it feel off the path. When the sheep was stuck. When a sheep had gone astray. It was a form of protection against the enemy.

The cross is our Shepherd's staff. It is how He rescued us from sin. How He pulled us out of our pits. How He found us when we went astray. How He protects us from the enemy. How He defeated death.

"Your rod and your staff, they comfort me."

Come alive at the cross today. It's a cross carried by a Shepherd who cares for His sheep. So much that He laid down His life. FOR YOU.

Psalm 18:16 says, "He sent from on high, he took me, he drew me out of many waters. He rescued me from my strong enemy and from those who hated me, for they were too mighty for me."

Even death could not defeat our Shepherd Jesus' staff, the cross.

Heart Work Day 16

Read It: Psalms 23
Say It: the whole passage just for kicks

Apply It:

Pray It:

Coming Alive Moments:

Heart Work Day 17

Read It: John 10
Say It: John 10:10

Apply It:

Pray It:

Coming Alive Moments:

Heart Work Day 18

Read It: John 11
Say It: John 11:40

Apply It:

Pray It:

Coming Alive Moments:

Heart Work Day 19

Read It: John 12
Say It: John 12:45-46

Apply It:

Pray It:

Coming Alive Moments:

Heart Work Day 20

Read It: John 13
Say It: John 13:34-35

Apply It:

Pray It:

Coming Alive Moments:

5 THE SAILOR

In the last chapter, we got excited together that Jesus is our shepherd. Well, at least I hope you got excited. There are a couple of times that I shouted, "Glory!" so I hope you wanted to, as well. As I write, I try to picture that I am having a conversation with you. Because I like people, and writing is well, a quiet activity. So when I am pretending you are here with me, the people in the coffee shop may wonder why I am letting out a little glory shout or a giggle now and then. Because well sometimes, I crack myself up. And I like to think you would be laughing with me.

I digress.

As I was praying about this next chapter, the Lord reminded me that not only was Jesus a shepherd, He was a sailor. He rode a boat or two in his ministry. He also called some disciples who made their living out of a boat to his ministry. So in this chapter, we are going to study how the Jesus who carried the cross for us also calmed some stormy seas as an example for us.

Airborne

My dad has been known to have some crazy ideas. They seem like good ideas at the time, but they usually involve some sort of fun family fiasco that creates an awesome memory but includes an unplanned adventure or two.

We have had a couple of different fishing boats over the years. And by we, I mean my parents—who were gracious enough to take us out on their various marine vessels. That sounds way more fancy than they really were—the term "marine vessels." It makes us sound like we were sailors on the open sea. Really they were passed down, used, halfway-broken-down boats on lakes that have a warning that you can only eat two catfish a year because of the radioactive material in the water from the nearby nuclear plant.

Just keeping it real here.

One of those boats we could call a speed boat. And to be honest, it was my least favorite boat. Contrary to what you would think, this girl who loves to travel the world as an adventurer does not like adventures.

I do not like things that go fast.

I rode the smallest roller coaster you can ride at Six Flags once. It was a kiddie roller coaster, and I was not a kid. But I turned into a child on that roller coaster. I was a crying mess. It was not a pretty picture. And I decided from then on that even standing in line for a roller coaster was like Chinese water torture. (For full disclosure, I am not even sure what Chinese water torture is, but that just seemed like a fitting word picture.) So you will not find me standing in line with you for the latest amusement park attraction. Sorry. I would love to have coffee with you in a nice, stable seat instead.

I digress.

One day we had the speed boat out on the Tennessee River very near the same area where they have the catfish eating warning. (PS: I have eaten more than two catfish from that river, just so you know.)

We heard there was a big steamboat from the Mississippi River that had floated down to our part of town. This was the old fashioned type of steamboat with the big pipe organ that plays the semi-off key music and has the real paddle wheel. My dad decided we needed to be close to that boat.

It really was fun. We pulled our little speed boat up right next to the big guy. It looked a bit like David next to Goliath. Or a life raft next to the Titanic.

It was fun while the boat was still. The paddle wheel was not moving, but the music was playing. The people were moving about. We just enjoyed watching this piece of history float nearby.

But then.

There tends to be those "but then" moments doesn't there?

But then the steamboat needed to turn around.

It was time to go against the current. To go back the other way. To do that, no longer would the big boat just idly float down river. The motor would need to be turned on, and the paddle wheel would need to start turning.

The BIG motor would need to be turned on, and the giant paddle wheel would need to start turning.

It happened in an instant. We were not expecting what happened next, because we were relaxing on our tiny speed boat enjoying the water and the scenery.

Once the engines were on and the boat turned, a huge wake started.

We were right in the middle of that big boat's wake. I was at the front of the boat with my sister. My dad and mom were in the back of the boat. It felt like when the Titanic started sinking. In a split second, the boat was literally airborne, the front of the boat going first.

My sister and I were caught off guard and found ourselves trying to cling to any part of the boat we could. The boat and my body were literally airborne. True confession, sometimes I exaggerate stories for dramatic effect, but you can ask any of the four of us on that boat that day. We were hurled into the air when we least expected it. No dramatic exaggeration necessary.

I remember desperately trying to cling to anything I could get my hands on in that boat as we hit the water again and flew airborne again and again.

I was not sure what was happening on the back of the boat, but based on my mom's panicked screams, it was something very similar to what was happening on the front of the boat.

In an instant, our peaceful ride had turned into a movie-worthy "will we make it through this or will we drown?" moment. We were all desperately trying to find something to hold onto.

Life has moments like this, or seasons like this, or sometimes even decades like this. Our normal mundane quickly turns into a nightmare of chaos. We suddenly find ourselves wondering if we will make it through this or will we drown.

It could be a financial storm where, all of a sudden, the bills come in, and you are buried underneath.

It could be an emotional storm where you can no longer contain your anxious thoughts. It could be that your struggle with depression has made your bed a place you cannot seem to crawl out of.

It could be a relational storm of betrayal, abuse, or disappointment.

It could be a spiritual storm where you cannot find even a mustard seed of faith to move the mountain.

You are in your "airborne." Like a trapeze artist flying through the air, searching for the next trapeze bar. Where can you find hope in the space in between?

Calm in the Storm

The disciples that hung out with Jesus had a few boat stories of their own. They were fishermen when Jesus found them after all. I just wonder what they were thinking when Jesus called to them and asked them to follow Him and be fishers of men (Matthew 4:18). There must have been something about this Jesus that convinced them, because it says they immediately left and followed Him. That is material for a whole different book.

There may not have been an old-fashioned steam boat found in their fishing stories, but there were some waves and some big storms.

Luke 8:22-25 tells one account of this storm story. The disciples and Jesus were in a boat and sailing away. Jesus must have found the water relaxing because He fell asleep. How amazing is it that the Jesus, who created this water, was in a boat sailing through it?

All of a sudden, a storm came up. Currently, as I am writing on a borrowed back porch (I don't have my own back porch, and I really like to write on back porches), there is a significant thunderstorm raging outside. The thunder just rattled my seat with its strength. A storm on the water takes things to a whole new level.

"As they sailed he fell asleep. And a windstorm came down on the lake, and they were filling with water and were in danger, and they went and woke him, saying, "Master, Master, we are perishing." (Luke 8:23-24)

"Perishing" is a pretty strong word to use folks. It's not just "we are a little bit scared, things are getting a little rocky here" fear. Perishing is the "I think I might not make it out of this storm" kind of fear.

Life storms can do that. All you can see in those moments are the wind and the waves. The way your heart is moving up and down and cannot seem to find a stable place to be still.

The way you cannot sleep at night with the anxious thoughts of what ifs and how come and what will happen next.

The way you wonder if you will ever make it out of this storm kind of fear, or the wondering if you even want to.

"I am airborne and desperately wanting to be on shore" moments.

The disciples called on Jesus in their despair in those storm moments. The waves were crashing over their boat, and they were not ready to drown. The Bible says in Luke 8:24

"He awoke and rebuked the wind and the raging waves and there was a calm."

They were still in the boat.

It does not say the rain stopped. It does not say they were magically transported out of the boat to the nice warm By the Seashore Five Star Seafood restaurant to have a six course meal like this had never happened.

But it does say there was a calm.

Chaos in our lives rudely breaks in. It often does not knock or wait to be invited. It breaks down the door, settles in, and says, "I am your uninvited guest." You may not be prepared for chaos to enter. You may not have had time to wash the sheets, get out the good china, and have everything in your house in order for this guest to arrive.

But we can invite calm in. Just like the disciples invited calm in on the stormy sea that day. They called to the One who was already in the boat with them to protect them in the storm.

Come

Jesus did not just always calm the seas. He also walked on the sea. Matthew 14 tells us Jesus had been busy doing the Jesus-y thing, ministering to the large crowds that had gathered. He sent the disciples away to go to the other side of the sea, and He stayed for a little while longer with the crowd. After dismissing the crowd a bit later, He went away by himself to pray.

In the fourth watch of the night, Jesus came to where the disciples were. He did not take the ordinary way. No boat for Jesus. He just decided to walk to them on the sea. You know, just another ordinary night, right?

Not really. I mean, I have not seen anyone walk on the water lately, have you?

I think I would have reacted the same way the disciples did in that moment. I would have wondered if I was seeing things. Is there such things as a ghost? Did what I eat for dinner have some sort of drug slipped into it?

Matthew 14:26 tells us the disciples were terrified and said, "It is a ghost!" and cried out in fear.

I love this next part. BUT immediately Jesus spoke to them saying, "Take heart, it is I. Do not be afraid."

I love that Jesus did not condemn their fear. He didn't mock them for being silly, scared boys. He immediately told them to not be afraid. He proclaimed who it was that was walking to them on the water.

The next part really does astound me. Good old Peter's response. He is quite the character. He said, "Well Jesus, if it is you, ask me to come to you on this water."

I wonder if he was secretly hoping the man walking towards them would cry out, "oh—ha, faked you out! I'm not Jesus at all."

Because this seemed like a pretty bold statement to me. If it's you, I am coming.

Guess what. Jesus said, "Come."

This is a short little sentence. Come. But wow, the impact this call to action had.

Jesus said, " Come" so Peter did. He got out of the boat and walked on the water.

ON THE WATER. I feel like we should remember some basic laws of science here, friends. Water is not for walking. Unless you have skis and are being pulled behind a boat.

I took a boat ride on the Sea of Galilee a few weeks ago. (I am not going to lie that it is super fun to say.) It was so amazing to be in the middle of that water, imagining that moment. This water does not have a secret walkway or reef. It is just like any other water. When you get in, you sink in.

Peter had a moment like we probably would. All of a sudden, he is realizing what he is doing. I am not on dry ground here people. I am not in the boat like my friends. I am on water and trying to walk.

Fear overtook him, and he began to sink.

Jesus has another immediate moment. He doesn't wait until Peter drowns and they have to call in Baywatch. He doesn't wait until Peter has sunk to the bottom forever.

He immediately reached out His hand. He reached out and took his hand. He kept him from sinking.

Jesus had said come and Peter went. And when he realized what he was really doing, trying to walk on water, he started to sink.

The One who had said, "Come" reached out and rescued the one who had stepped out.

Jesus calls us to come.

> *Matthew 11:28, "Come to me all you who are weary and heavy laden and I will give you rest."*

He also says in Matthew 16:24, *"If anyone would come after me, let him deny himself and take up his cross and follow me."*

Jesus took up His cross so we could follow Him with ours.

He calls us to come when we are tired. He calls us to come when we are scared. He calls us to come when what He is calling us to may seem impossible.

The only way I can find the obedience to come when He calls is when I think about how He came for me. He came from heaven to earth.

I want to be a Peter. When God calls me to Him, I want to come.

When He calls me to be used by Him, I want to come.

When He calls me to walk on water for Him, I want to get out of the boat and walk on that water.

And when I start to sink in fear, I want to call out to Him. I would much rather have His hand catch me while I am sinking than be in the boat watching.

What is Jesus calling you to?

Come.

Heart Work Day 21

Read It: Matthew 14:22-34
Say It: Matthew 14:28-32
Apply It:

Pray It:

Coming Alive Moments:

Heart Work Day 22

Read It: Mark 6:30-56
Say It: Mark 6:50-52
Apply It:

Pray It:

Coming Alive Moments:

Heart Work Day 23

Read It: Luke 9:10-27
Say It: Luke 9:23
Apply It:

Pray It:

Coming Alive Moments:

Heart Work Day 24

Read It: John 14
Say It: John 14:16-17

Apply It:

Pray It:

Coming Alive Moments:

Heart Work Day 25

Read It: John 15
Say It: John 15:9-11

Apply It:

Pray It:

Coming Alive Moments:

6 BROKEN BREAD AND BETRAYAL

I love communion. The Lord's Supper. The breaking of the bread and the drinking of the juice. I have taken it in all kinds of different churches in all kinds of different ways. Each significant. I pray I never take lightly the gift of taking communion in remembrance of the One who allowed His life to be taken for me.

I have only had the chance to serve communion once. Can I let you in on a little secret? I was scared to death. I had grown up in the "pass the silver tray full of the grape juice cups (passing those is QUITE the balancing act) and the silver plate with the tiny wafers" church. I like to refer to that as the "swallowing the pill" method.

I love the rip and dip method myself. Something about tearing off that piece of bread and dipping helps me identify with Christ's body torn for me.

This particular time, I was working at a camp, and the camp director had asked me to be one of the ones who held the cup and served the juice as people walked through the line.

I was supposed to hold the cup and repeat a simple phrase. "This is the blood of Jesus shed for you" to each person as they dipped.

Did I mention I was nervous? I just did not want to get this holy act wrong. Everything was going ok until it came time for my boss to go through my line. I was all nervous and tongue tied. Ok, here is a little warning for you—this was not my most spiritual moment, and if you have water in your mouth, you may spit it out laughing--consider yourself forewarned.

I got tongue tied and I said to my boss, " This is the boob of

Jesus shed for you."

Not blood. This is not a type-o. I said boob. This was not the serving communion, holy moment I was hoping for.

I am turning beat red and sweating just thinking about it. He had NO idea how to respond, and I didn't either. I did the only thing I knew to do. I shouted, "I mean the blood, not the boob."

Needless to say, I felt like in that moment, my communion-serving moments were over.

Jesus' time with the disciples in the last supper was a holy moment. They had gathered in the upper room to observe the Passover feast.

Luke 22:17-21 tells us Jesus said something that the disciples were not expecting.

"And he took bread, and when he had given thanks, he broke it and gave it to them, saying, 'This is my body, which is given for you. Do this in remembrance of me.' And likewise, the cup after they had eaten saying, 'This cup that is poured out for you is the new covenant in my blood.'"

Can you imagine having dinner with your closest friends and family? You have gotten together for Thanksgiving feast. You are ready to bless the food. Then your grandpa stands up with a roll and said, "This is my body broken for you. This sweet tea represents my blood that will be shed for you."

What would your response be?

Jesus knew this would be his last big meal with his disciples. The ones who had left everything to follow Him. He knew the significance of this moment. He wanted them to be ready for what was to come.

And He wants us to do this in remembrance of Him. Because of what was proclaimed during communion in the upper room that day, we get to commune with Jesus today.

Jesus knew His blood must flow so that His grace could flow.

Jesus knew His body must be broken so we could be made whole.

Jesus also knew that He was breaking bread with the one who would betray Him.

Betrayal.

When I really let my heart meditate on this, it amazes me the love Jesus had. He broke bread with one He knew would betray Him.

I do not pick friends hoping one of them will betray me. I do not say, "Hey, pass the bread, and by the way, I am so glad that you are here with us tonight because you are going to deliver me to death tomorrow."

But Jesus did. He invited Judas to the table.

Matthew 26:23, "He who has dipped his hand in this dish with me will betray me."

How is that for dinner-stopping conversation?

Jesus invited the betrayer to the table. He invites me to the table. He invites you to the table.

My sin betrays Jesus.

Romans 3:23, "For all have sinned and fallen short of the glory of God." But yet He invites me to the table. Come alive at the communion table today.

In the Garden

Jesus left the Upper Room for a garden. The Garden of Gethsemane. This was a very significant moment leading to the cross. Here, in this garden, Jesus cried out in prayer.

He knew what was to come. He knew the suffering ahead. He knew He was taking on the weight of the sin of the world. He was in such intense prayer, He sweat drops of blood in that garden. His soul was in agony about what was to come.

But He chose to take on the cross.

Have you ever thought about before how sin first entered the world in a garden, and Jesus agreed to take on the sins of the world in a garden?

Adam and Eve chose to disobey God by eating of the tree of the knowledge of good and evil in the Garden of Eden, causing sin to enter the world.

Jesus chose to obey God by drinking of the cup of suffering, providing a rescue from sin in the world.

Matthew 26:42, "My Father, if this cannot pass unless I drink it, your will be done."

Your. Will. Be Done. He chose this for me and for you.

Mt. Precipice

We drove our tour bus (well, I didn't drive...I happily rode in the tour bus) into Nazareth. I could not believe that I was in the town where Jesus grew up. I could just imagine him roaming these streets. Imagine what it was like for Mary that day, when an angel showed up announcing she would be the mother of the Son of God.

We drove up a very windy road and parked on Mt. Precipice. Truthfully, I was not sure what in the Bible had happened here. That was a constant question in my mind as we drove around Israel. What happened here?

We hiked up until we were on a cliff, overlooking the city of Nazareth. As we were looking out in Nazareth, deep in the valley below, the guide began to read from Luke 4:28. Honestly I don't recall having ever noticed this story in the Bible before. But standing on the spot where it happened, it held a huge meaning to me.

Apparently the people in Jesus' hometown were not loving him. They were not liking His teachings, or who He claimed to be.

Luke 4:28-29 tells us, "When they heard these things, all in the synagogue were filled with wrath. And they rose up and drove him out of the town and brought him to the brow of the hill of which their town was built, so that they could throw him down the cliff. But passing through their midst, he went away."

They had all the intentions to kill Jesus that day. As I stood there, I realized it would have been a very difficult place to escape from. There was really no way around but down. If they threw him off the cliff as they had planned, He would quickly perish.

But it was not his time.

So He passed through their midst. I do not know if that means He disappeared, or somehow sneaked among those in the crowd, or if an angel covered Him in a cloud of glory.

But I do know, the plans of man to kill him were not accomplished that day. It was not the timing of the Lord.

Now, let's go back to the Garden of Gethsemane. As I was sitting in that Garden imagining Jesus sweating drops of blood for me, I realized there were so many places He could have escaped to. It would have been very easy for Him to again "pass through their midst." When He saw the soldiers coming, He could have escaped into the town.

But He chose. He chose to stay. He chose to pray. He chose to obey.

It was His time. He knew the suffering that was coming. The shame of the cross. The pain of the cross. The weight of the sin on the cross.

And He said, "Yes." He said yes because He loves you. Because He loves me. He wants nothing to separate us from the Love of God in Christ Jesus.

Come alive at the choice Jesus made to suffer the cross today.

Heart Work Day 26

Read It: John 16
Say It: John 16:25-32
Apply It:

Pray It:

Coming Alive Moments:

Heart Work Day 27

Read It: John 17
Say It: John 17:20-23
Apply It:

Pray It:

Coming Alive Moments:

Heart Work Day 28

Read It: Luke 22
Say It: Luke 22:19-23
Apply It:

Pray It:

Coming Alive Moments:

Heart Work Day 29

Read It: Mark 14
Say It: Mark 14:34-36
Apply It:

Pray It:

Coming Alive Moments:

Heart Work Day 30

Read It: Matthew 26:1-56
Say It: Matthew 26:42

Apply It:

Pray It:

Coming Alive Moments:

7 HIS DEATH MY LIFE

The soldiers came and found Jesus in the Garden as Judas betrayed Jesus with a kiss. They captured Jesus and led him to Caiaphas's house. He was the high priest, and they wanted him to tell them what to do with Jesus.

I stood at the steps of Caiaphas's house. There was nothing remarkably different inside. Until they told us they were taking us into the place in the house where prisoners were held in this house. It was in the dungeon of the basement. Jesus would have likely been held overnight as they prepared to turn him over to Pilate, the governor.

This was no dungeon. This was a pit. Deep underground. It took my breath away as we walked deeper and deeper into that pit. That small underground area. There would have been no stairs and no lights. My Jesus would have been lowered into this pit and bound there in complete darkness.

Have you ever been in complete darkness? I used to lead caving trips when I was a camp counselor. I had to pretend that I loved them because that was the camp counselor thing to do, but truthfully, there was nothing about caving that I liked.

Small, dark, damp, muddy spaces were not my idea of a grand time.

There was a time in the cave when we would have all of our campers turn off their lights so they could experience absolute darkness. Jesus was willing to experience such absolute darkness for us. Darkness in the dungeon that night. Darkness on the cross the next day. Three days of darkness in the grave.

He went into that pit so that we never have to stay bound in a pit of darkness.

Galatians 5:1 says, "If the Son has set you free, you are FREE indeed."

"I am counted among those who go down to the pit, I am a man who has no strength, like one set loose among the dead, like the slain that lie in the grave, like those you remember no more. You have put me in the depths of the pit, in the regions dark and deep. Your wrath lies heavy upon me." (Psalm 88:4-7)

Jesus was counted among those who go down to the pit, letting God's wrath lie heavy upon Him so God's wrath could be lifted off of me.

Whew. That's so much to take in.

The enemy of our souls would like for us to stay in our pits. Our pits of sin. Our pits of self-pity. Our pits of despair. Our pits of bondage. Of making the same bad decision over and over. Our pit of desire for love. Our pit of failure.

There is deep darkness in a pit.

But we have a Savior who rescues us from our pits.

"Surely he has borne our griefs and carried our sorrows; yet we esteemed him stricken, smitten by God and afflicted. But He was wounded for our transgressions; he was crushed for our iniquities; upon him was the chastisement that brought us peace, and with his stripes we are healed." (Isaiah 53:4-5)

With His stripes, we are healed.

Jesus went from Caiaphas to Pilate. He was beaten. He was mocked. He was paraded before the people. The King of Kings was mocked as a false king of the Jews. The crowds who had been shouting, "Hosanna" were now crying, "Crucify Him."

With a robe and a crown, He carried a cross to Golgotha. This place is called "the place of a skull" due to the skull formation in the rock. The One who formed that rock was to be crucified on a cross on the rock.

It is Finished

These three words. It is finished. Just three simple words. But these words said by Jesus on the cross, recorded in John 19:30, are turning-point words.

These words change our lives. After Jesus said, "It is finished," John 19:30 says,

"He bowed his head and gave up his spirit."

What was finished? The end of this story was the beginning of our stories. His work on the cross was done, and resurrection was coming soon.

In that moment on the cross, Jesus was telling us that all the ways of the old covenant were finished. No longer do we have to go wait in line at the temple, bringing our sacrifice to find forgiveness of sins.

No longer do we need a priest to go into the Holy of Holies at the temple on the Day of Atonement to ask for our atonement.

Our need to have it all together was finished. Our need to be perfect was finished that day by the Perfect One.

The veil in the temple was torn in two.

I wonder how the disciples felt that day, hearing Jesus utter those words. They were watching the One they had followed as a Messiah die an excruciating death on a cross like a common criminal. They had not yet experienced the hope of Resurrection Sunday.

They were watching the end of the life of the One they had left everything to follow.

Was their hope finished? Was who they had left their lives to follow worth it?

The enemy wants us to think our hope is finished. When we make bad decisions. When we experience devastating hurts. When we are walking in shame and condemnation.

When our families are not walking in the truth. When our friends betray us. When we fail. When we get angry. When are life plans are not turning out the way we expected. When our lives' plans are going as we expected but not living up to our expectations.

Have you experienced the enemy telling you hope is finished? His accusing tone telling you that you should have never stood on hope in the first place?

Jesus was not declaring that hope was finished that day when He breathed His last.

He was declaring the power of sin and death was finished. Defeated. The redemption plan set in motion in the Garden of Eden had been accomplished. Hope was not finished, but death was.

Waiting

Raise your hand if you like waiting in lines? Being put on hold when you are on the phone, especially when they play really awesome hold music? Waiting for your appointment, and the doctor is two hours late?

We are not really a people who like to wait.

Waiting requires a stillness, a pause, an in between.

What are you currently waiting for? There was a three-day pause between death and life. The redemption plan was finished, but the resurrection story was coming. In the waiting, God was working. He is always working behind the scenes.

In your in-between, know that the same God that brought Jesus from death to life is working behind the scenes. He is working in your story. He has not forgotten you. He will not leave you. He is with you. And He is working a new life into your story.

Isaiah 40:31 says, "Those who wait for the Lord shall renew their strength; they shall mount up on wings like eagles, they shall run and not be weary, they shall walk and not faint."

We celebrate Good Friday. Truthfully, there would be NOTHING good about the Friday Jesus died on the cross if it were not for the promise of Sunday.

In the waiting, God was working. He was getting ready to burst forth on the scene.

Come alive today watching for Him to burst forth on your scene.

"Having the eyes of your heart enlightened, that you may know what is the hope to which he has called you, what are the riches of his glorious inheritance in the saints, and what is the immeasurable greatness of His power toward us, who believe, according to his great might, that he worked in Christ when He raised him from the dead and seated him at his right hand in the heavenly places." (Ephesians 1:18-20)

Heart Work Day 31

Read It: Matthew 26:57-75
Say It: Matthew 26:64

Apply It:

Pray It:

Coming Alive Moments:

Heart Work Day 32

Read It: John 18
Say It: John 18:7-8

Apply It:

Pray It:

Coming Alive Moments:

Heart Work Day 33

Read It: John 19
Say It: John 19:30

Apply It:

Pray It:

Coming Alive Moments:

Heart Work Day 34

Read It: Luke 23
Say It: Luke 23:46

Apply It:

Pray It:

Coming Alive Moments:

Heart Work Day 35

Read It: Luke 23:44-55
Say It: Luke 23:46

Apply It:

Pray It:

Coming Alive Moments:

8 HE CAME ALIVE

I am not really sure how to start the first paragraph of the last chapter of this book. That seems like a fairly good way to start when you are having a hard time figuring out how to close. I want to have a funny story. I want it to be something that you remember. That sticks with you. But all I can do, as I sit here and type, is want to shout, "Glory!"

It's Easter Sunday. This is the day that I was originally planning to have this book released. Obviously, I am still working on it because God changed so much of it while I was in Israel. There are forty five more minutes left on this Easter Sunday before it becomes Monday. (Yes, I am up late. Too much coffee and Easter Candy).

Celebrating Easter Sunday is such a great moment in the life of a Christian. But truthfully, every day is Easter.

He is alive. He came alive, and therefore, you and I get to live alive in Christ.

Those days of waiting—when Jesus was in the grave—were dark days. Days when God's work on the earth seemed quiet and over.

But God.

But God is a promise-keeper. He promised Abraham He would make his descendants like the sand on the seashore, and He did. Even when it seemed impossible because Abraham was ancient and almost ready for the assisted living home and still had no child.

God is a promise-keeper and was working in the waiting.

He promised David that the Messiah would come from His family line. And He did.

Jesus promised Martha in John 11:25 that He was the resurrection and the life. And He was.

Matthew 28 is one of the most exciting passages in the Bible. In Matthew 28, we find Mary Magdalene and "the other Mary" (lots of Mary's in the Bible, folks) are going to see the tomb.

When they got there, they experienced a very dramatic scene. An earthquake and an angel. Not something that happens every day.

I love this next part. I really want to almost write it in all caps, but I am sure that is against some sort of grammar rule. So just now, I am typing these keys with excitement. I hope you read this with excitement. No matter how many times you have heard it, would you read this as if it the first time you are reading it?

We should be the most excited people on the planet when we think about this.

Matthew 28:5 says, "But the angel said to the women, 'Do not be afraid, for I know that you seek Jesus WAS crucified. He is not here, for He has risen, as He said.'"

Ok, let's put some emphasis on some exciting words here.

Jesus WAS crucified. He was. It happened. He hung on the cross. He was dead.

But, he is NOT here.

Nope. Not here. Not in this tomb. Let's read that again. NOT HERE. He was dead, but He lives.

Just as He said.

He is a promise-keeper my friends.

The same Jesus who promised to come back to life and did is keeping His promises to you.

Can you just take a moment and worship the Resurrected King? The One who does what He says. The One who defeated death. The One who defeated the enemy.

"O death, where is your victory O death, where is your sting?" (1 Corinthians 15:55)

GLOOORRRRY!!!! (Sorry, I could not hold it in any longer!) We can come alive at the cross today because He came alive after the cross.

That resurrection power can resurrect me. And you.
"If anyone is in Christ He is a new creation, the old has gone the new has come." (2 Corinthians 5:17)

So What?

My pastor, Jon Teague, ends all of his sermons with this question: "So What?" I love that. It's a way for us to take all the information we have learned and think about how it will become a transformation in our lives.

So what? So Jesus came back to life just as He said. Jesus is alive. So how does that impact our lives?

Jesus made sure to give the disciples some parting lines before He ascended into heaven. I felt the Holy Spirit impress upon me to remind us of these words as we think about how His coming alive should impact our lives.

Jesus gave a charge, a commission, to the disciples who had been with Him on the journey from His earthly ministry, to His death, to the waiting, to the praising that He had risen just as He said.

"Go therefore and make disciples of all nations, baptizing them in the name of the Father and of the Son and of the Holy Spirit, teaching them to observe all that I have commanded you. And behold, I am with you always to the end of the age." (Matthew 28:19-20)

My friend, He is with you ALWAYS.

So let's go. Let's live so alive in Christ that people want to know the Christ that we know.

Let's make disciples. Let's be disciples. Because He is with us. He is in us. And He lives through us.

"It is no longer I who live, but Christ who lives in me. And the life I now live in the flesh I live by faith in the Son of God who loved me and gave himself for me." (Galatians 2:20)

Thanks for joining the Coming Alive at the Cross adventure. It is my prayer that you were forever changed. I believe YOU were in the right place at the right time, and that God brought you here. (Go ahead and giggle as you remember that story from Chapter 1).

May I have the joy of praying over you?

Father I pray for each person that took this journey. Who said yes. Who came. Jesus would you change us forever as recognize the power of the cross. I pray we got to know you better as we studying not just what you did for us, but who you were.

Jesus I pray for each of my new friends. I pray that they will cling to you in the common, the chaos, and the calm. But above all else, they will know that you are clinging to them. With the power of the cross.

. Jesus I pray for the glory of this story to come alive in new ways.

For the power of the cross to flow into our daily mundane. For you to show us that resurrection power. Thank you that the same power that raised Jesus from the dead is available to us, as you promise in Ephesians 1:19-20.

I confess you as my Savior. I celebrate that you have chosen to pour out your grace and love on me. And I ask your forgiveness for the ways in which I forget. Forgive me for not letting the story of the resurrection impact every part of my story.

You are faithful and you are true. Father meet us in our day to day. Remind us our your new mercies for us – today and tomorrow. Thank you that you are always the same. That your love never changes. Today we celebrate that in the waiting you are working. Help us to worship while we wait. Help us to cling to the promise of heaven while our feet still walk this earth.

Thank you that you are risen, just as you said!

In Jesus Name,
Amen

Heart Work Day 36

Read It: Luke 24:1-50
Say It: Luke 24:36-44

Apply It:

Pray It:

Coming Alive Moments:

Heart Work Day 37

Read It: Matthew 28

Say It: Let's be crazy. There is so much power in this chapter. Would you be willing to read the whole chapter out loud? Grab another cup of coffee if you need to.

Apply It:

Pray It:

Coming Alive Moments:

Heart Work Day 38

Read It: Mark 16
Say It: Mark 16:15-19

Apply It:

Pray It:

Coming Alive Moments:

Heart Work Day 39

Read It: John 20
Say It: John 20:20-23

Apply It:

Pray It:

Coming Alive Moments

Heart Work Day 40

Read It: John 21
Say It: John 19:15-19

Apply It:

Pray It:

Coming Alive Moments:

ABOUT JENN

Jenn Hand is a strong coffee drinking lover of Jesus. She has a zest for life and loves to go on adventure with Jesus around the world — often getting lost somewhere along the way.

Jenn started her love of speaking and teaching the word of God when she got her first Precious Moments Bible at the age of eight years old when she accepted Christ's invitation to life. She used to have her friends gather on the playground and come to her Bible club.

Jenn has a Master's Degree in professional counseling from Richmont University and although not in private practice, loves to apply the things she learned as she helps you come alive.

Jenn has been professionally speaking since 2004 and became the Executive Director and founder of Coming Alive Ministries in 2012. She spent two life changing years overseas in South Asia as a missionary and has traveled to 22 countries to share the love of Jesus.

Jenn is an identical twin, and one of her favorite things is spoiling her nieces and nephew rotten. Jenn has served in a variety of areas including as a Baptist Collegiate Ministries director at Lee University, Women at the Well Ministries, ABWE missionary, and now as Executive Director and Keynote speaker for Coming Alive Ministries. She has spoken at hundreds of conferences and retreats, camps and ladies night out events, nationally and internationally.

She loves to laugh until she cries and believes the joy of the Lord is her strength. Jenn would love to connect with you and your group, inviting you to come alive with her.

You can connect with Jenn at www.comingaliveministries.com,
by e-mailing comingaliveministries@gmail.com.
Facebook www.facebook.com/comingaliveministries
or on Twitter and Instagram as @comingalivejenn

ABOUT COMING ALIVE MINISTRIES

Coming Alive Ministries was officially founded in May of 2012 as a dream and a calling to provide an invitation to Come Alive in Christ. Jenn Hand, Executive Director and founder of Coming Alive Ministries, returned home after living overseas for two years as a missionary in a country where people worshiped idols and statues all around her.

As Jenn returned home, she found herself traveling and speaking to churches about her experiences serving overseas. She began to notice church pews packed with people who said they knew the living God, but were living dead inside.

Coming Alive Ministries was founded as a 501 (c)3 organization to provide an invitation to come alive in Christ through conferences, retreats and written resources.

If you are interesting in book Jenn for a speaker, hosting a Bloom conference, or having Coming Alive Ministries minister to your missionaries/nationals overseas please contact us at www.comingaliveministries.com
   e-mail comingaliveministries@gmail.com

Made in the USA
San Bernardino, CA
13 August 2016